The Emergency Medical Services Workforce Agenda for the Future

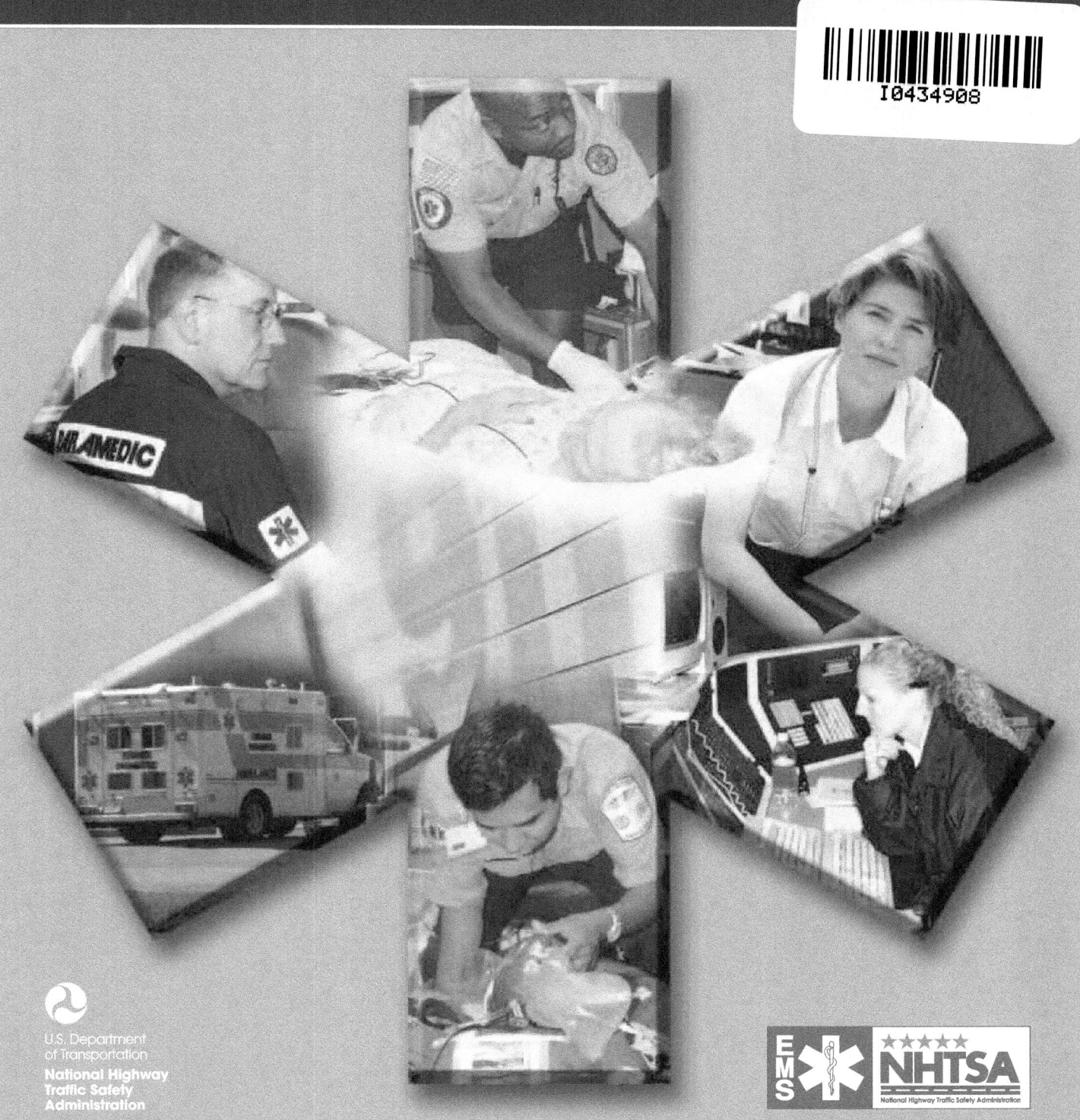

U.S. Department
of Transportation

**National Highway
Traffic Safety
Administration**

EMS NHTSA
National Highway Traffic Safety Administration

Prepared by:

University of California San Francisco (UCSF) Center for the Health Professions

Susan A. Chapman, PhD, RN
Assistant Professor, Dept. of Social and Behavioral Sciences, School of Nursing, Director of Allied Health Workforce Studies

Vanessa Lindler, MA
Senior Research Associate

Jennifer A. Kaiser, BA
Program Analyst

Reviewed by:

National Highway Traffic Safety Administration (NHTSA)
Office of Emergency Medical Services

Drew Dawson
Director

Gamunu Wijetunge, MPM, NREMT-P
EMS Specialist

Gerald Poplin, MS
Public Health Fellow

Steering Committee

John Becknell
Roger Levine, PhD
Gregg Margolis, PhD, NREMT-P
Richard Patrick, M.S., CFO, EMT-P
Jane Smith, NREMT-P
Ellen Weber, MD
Ed Wetzel

Funded by:

NHTSA
Health Resources and Services Administration (HRSA) Emergency Medical Services for
  Children (EMS-C) Program

Acknowledgements:

Thank you to John Becknell, Steering Committee Member, who was instrumental in the conceptual development and writing of this agenda.

DISCLAIMER:

This publication was prepared by UCSF through cooperative agreement DTNH22-04-H-05193. This publication is distributed by the U.S. Department of Transportation, National Highway Traffic Safety Administration, in the interest of information exchange. The opinions, findings, and conclusions expressed in this publication are those of the author(s) and not necessarily those of the Department of Transportation or the National Highway Traffic Safety Administration. The United States Government assumes no liability for its contents or use thereof. If trade or manufacturers' names or products are mentioned, it is because they are considered essential to the object of the publication and should not be construed as an endorsement. The United States Government does not endorse products or manufacturers.

TABLE OF CONTENTS

Executive Summary 1

Introduction 2

Vision, Purpose, and Components of the Agenda 3

   Vision 3

   Purpose 3

   Components of the EMS Workforce Agenda 3

A National Assessment of the EMS Workforce 7

   Data 7

   Education and Certification 7

   Recruitment and Retention 8

   Management 8

   Rural and Volunteer EMS Workforce 9

   Health and Safety 9

   Compensation: Pay and Benefits 9

   Professional Identity and Status 10

Components of the EMS Workforce Agenda 11

   Health, Safety, and Wellness 12

      Where We Are 12

      Where We Want To Be In 2020 13

      How to Get There 14

   Education and Certification 18

      Where We Are 18

      Where We Want To Be In 2020 19

      How to Get There 19

   Data and Research 22

      Where We Are 22

      Where We Want To Be In 2020 23

      How to Get There 24

Workforce Planning and Development..26

    Where We Are 26

    Where We Want To Be In 2020 27

    How to Get There..29

Technical Assistance and a Systems Approach to the EMS Workforce 30

Conclusion 32

Appendix A – Attendees at EMS Workforce Stakeholders Meeting..........33

References...35

EXECUTIVE SUMMARY

Emergency medical services (EMS) workers serve on the front lines of emergency medical care. The EMS system is vitally dependent on the ability of these workers to provide high-quality emergent health care in dynamic and oftentimes dangerous circumstances. In the community-based EMS system envisioned in the 1996 *EMS Agenda for the Future,* EMS workers would contribute to the health of the populations they serve by providing services that reflect the integration of EMS with other health care providers, and in other arenas, such as public health and public safety.

The Emergency Medical Services Workforce Agenda for the Future (EMS Workforce Agenda) envisions a future in which all EMS systems have a sufficient number of well educated, adequately prepared, and appropriately credentialed EMS workers who are valued, well compensated, healthy, and safe.

The *EMS Workforce Agenda* identifies the following four components critical to developing an EMS workforce that will thrive and be a driving force for achieving integrated, community-based EMS systems:

- health, safety and wellness of the EMS workforce.
- education and certification
- data and research
- workforce planning and development

The *EMS Workforce Agenda* also proposes the establishment of a National EMS Workforce Technical Assistance Center (TAC), whose function will be to assist national, state, territorial, tribal, local, and private EMS stakeholders with workforce development.

The vision of the *EMS Workforce Agenda* is ambitious but achievable with the continued collaboration of local, tribal, territorial, State, national and Federal EMS stakeholders.

INTRODUCTION

A principal component of any EMS system is its workforce. The ability of an EMS system to deliver high quality prehospital emergency care depends upon a qualified and capable workforce. However, in the past 40 years of modern EMS, clinical care issues have dominated the research literature, with little attention paid to the workforce beyond its education and training. As a result, the understanding of workforce issues and methods that attempt to address these issues vary greatly across both state and local levels. While some EMS systems appear to have been successful in meeting their workforce needs, there is currently no broad national effort to develop, identify, or share best practices in recruitment, retention, health and safety, or other EMS workforce issues.

In recent years, awareness of the urgency of EMS workforce issues has increased. Media and anecdotal reports of EMS worker shortages, problems with recruitment and retention, declining volunteerism, low worker pay and poor employment benefits, and concerns about worker health and safety issues has raised uncertainty about the viability of the workforce. At the same time recent national disasters have brought new attention to the vital roles EMS workers play in community health and public safety.

For many localities, the need for EMS is perceived to be increasing. EMS workers and industry leaders believe that urgent action is needed to ensure enough qualified future EMS workers. As the nation confronts an older and increasingly diverse population, overall workforce shortages, and the potential for global events such as pandemic influenza, it has become clear that increased efforts must be devoted to assuring EMS workforce viability.

VISION, PURPOSE, AND COMPONENTS OF THE AGENDA

Vision

EMS systems of the future will be able to recruit and maintain a sufficient number of well educated, adequately prepared, and appropriately credentialed EMS workers who are valued, well compensated, healthy, and safe.

Purpose

The *EMS Workforce Agenda for the Future (EMS Workforce Agenda)* builds on the findings of the recently published *EMS Workforce for the 21st Century: A National Assessment (EMS Workforce Assessment)*. The purpose of the *EMS Workforce Agenda* is to provide a vision for the future and to suggest strategies to help ensure a robust and capable EMS workforce in the 21st century.

Components of the EMS Workforce Agenda

The *EMS Workforce Agenda* depicts the essential components of: (1) workforce health, safety, and wellness; (2) education and certification; (3) data and research, and (4) workforce planning and development. The successful implementation of the *EMS Workforce Agenda* depends upon a coordinated systems approach involving the efforts of national, state, and local EMS agencies, in addition to a variety of stakeholder organizations. A proposed National EMS Workforce Technical Assistance Center (TAC) will help coordinate these efforts by collecting and disseminating EMS workforce best practices, promoting EMS workforce research, and providing EMS workforce technical assistance to local, state, and federal EMS agencies. A summary of the essential components of the *EMS Workforce Agenda* is included here.

Health, Safety, and Wellness – Support for the collection of workforce illness and injury data through a national EMS Workforce Injury and Illness Surveillance Program (EMS-WIISP)[3] is needed to ensure a healthy and safe workforce in the future. Data collected through the EMS-WIISP will provide the foundation for evidence-based safety standards, operational practices, and prevention strategies that promote and foster a culture of safety in EMS.

Education and Certification – High quality EMS education is needed to develop EMS personnel who are capable of delivering high quality prehospital health care. The education and certification components delineated in this document are based on the *EMS Education Agenda for the Future: A Systems Approach* (*EMS Education Agenda*).[2] The *EMS Education Agenda* has the overarching objective of improving the efficiency of the national EMS education process through development of five interdependent components: (1) the National EMS Core Content; (2) the National EMS Scope of Practice Model; (3) the National EMS Education Standards; (4) National EMS Education Program Accreditation, and (5) National EMS Certification. The *EMS Education Agenda* calls for all states to adopt National EMS Certification as the basis for EMS licensure, as well as national accreditation of all EMS education programs.

Data and Research – Current and accurate EMS workforce data and research are necessary to facilitate effective, evidence-based workforce planning. Action is necessary to cultivate a robust body of EMS workforce research. The national EMS community needs to develop an integrated system of uniform workforce data collection. Pertinent data on the EMS workforce, including compensation, the number of paid and volunteer workers, and the number of enrollees and graduates of education programs, should regularly be collected at the local and state levels and reported nationally.

Workforce Planning and Development – An evidence-based approach to EMS workforce planning and development is needed to predict the future supply of EMS workers and the demand for their services across the range of geographic service areas. All levels of EMS will benefit from taking a proactive approach to meeting future demand for workers, including volunteers. To be effective, workforce planning and development will require access to current and accurate EMS workforce data.

National EMS Workforce Technical Assistance Center (TAC) – Given the diversity of EMS systems in the United States, advancing and promoting the essential components of the *EMS Workforce Agenda* will require coordination among national, state, territorial, tribal, local and private EMS stakeholders. A proposed National EMS Workforce Technical Assistance Center (TAC) would facilitate the efforts of EMS stakeholders which may include, but are not limited to, the following:

- EMS workers
- Consumers, including adults, children, and various special needs populations
- EMS employers
- State EMS offices
- Local and tribal EMS systems and provider agencies
- Certification and accreditation organizations
- Standards setting organizations
- Education programs and institutions
- National, state, and local EMS organizations
- Federal EMS agencies
- Public health agencies
- Rural health agencies
- Private EMS providers
- Other non-governmental organizations

Figure 1. Essential Components of the EMS Workforce Agenda

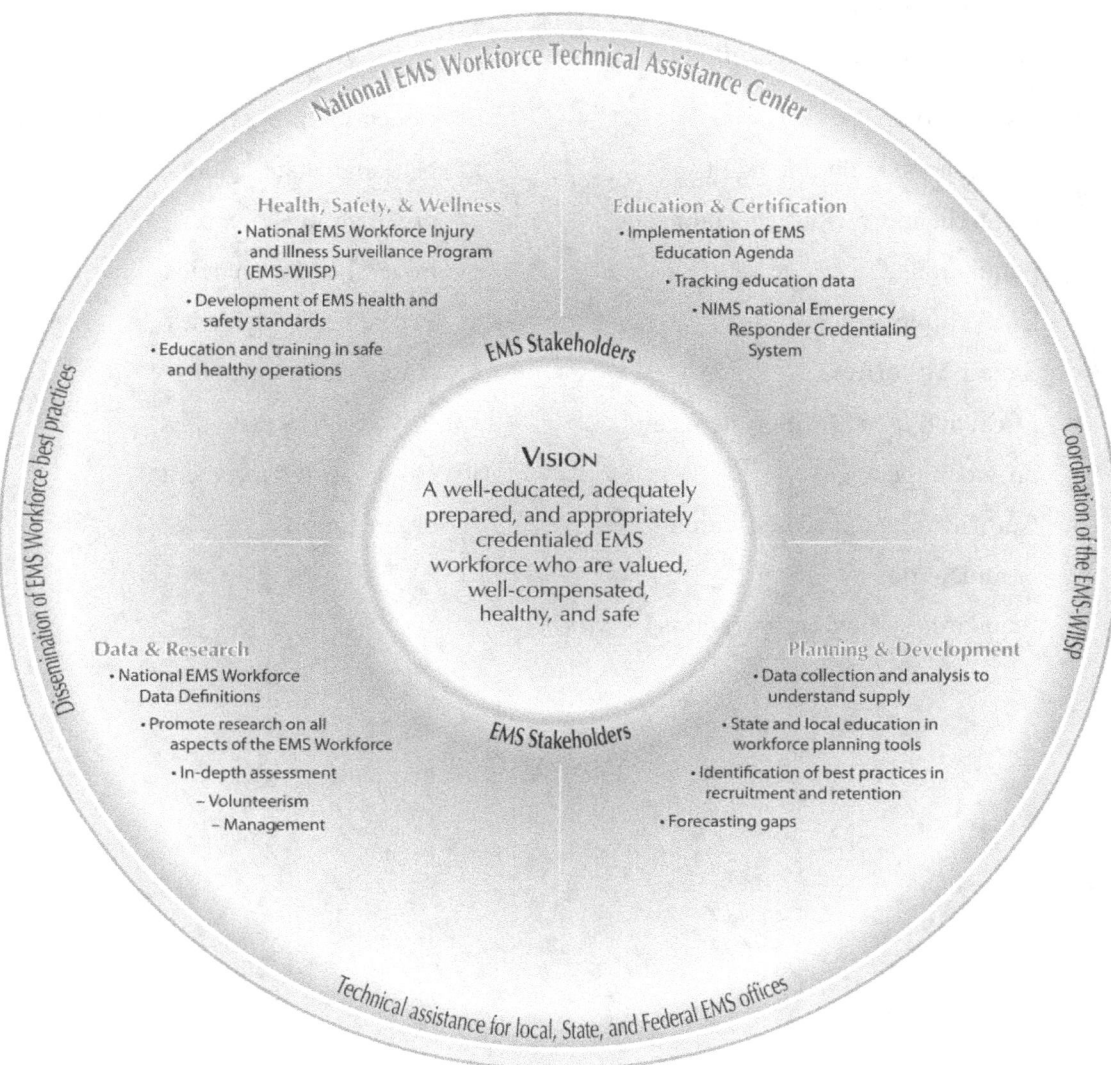

Essential Components of the EMS Workforce Agenda for the Future

Figure 1 depicts the essential components of the *EMS Workforce Agenda* and their relationship to stakeholders, the TAC and the vision of the future EMS workforce.

A NATIONAL ASSESSMENT OF THE EMS WORKFORCE

In response to a growing EMS community interest in ensuring a robust and capable workforce, NHTSA initiated a national EMS workforce project in 2005. The first step of the EMS Workforce for the 21st Century Project (Workforce Project) was a systematic and in-depth assessment of the national EMS workforce, including primary data collection, a synthesis of existing data and research, and the input of key EMS workforce experts and national stakeholders. The findings of *EMS Workforce for the 21st Century: A National Assessment* [4] (*EMS Workforce Assessment*), are summarized by the following critical issues:

Data

An important finding from the *EMS Workforce Assessment* is that much of the data necessary for evaluating the adequacy of EMS workforce supply is either not collected or has substantial limitations that impede its use in workforce planning. The most basic workforce statistics, such as workforce size, cannot be accurately estimated using available data. National sources of workforce data do not account for the complexities of the EMS workforce. For example, the Bureau of Labor Statistics' Occupational Employment Statistics program (BLS-OES) database does not distinguish between EMTs and paramedics, does not identify EMTs cross-trained as firefighters, and does not capture volunteer EMS workers. Estimates of the size of the EMS workforce reported from BLS-OES data are underestimated by an unknown amount. The inability to accurately estimate EMS workforce size is a fundamental problem for EMS workforce planning and will hamper the ability to anticipate future EMS workforce needs.

Education and Certification

Certification and licensure requirements for EMS workers create a confusing picture due to differing types and levels of certification and licensure available across the states. Furthermore, data on the emerging workforce (e.g. student and educational programs) are also limited. For example, the U.S. Department of Education's National Center for Education Statistics (NCES), does not distinguish between EMT and paramedic education programs and does not capture data from all educational programs. Another source of educational programs data, the American Medical Association (AMA), only collects data from accredited paramedic programs and does not collect data from EMT programs. The lack of complete data about students in the EMS educational pipeline hinders efforts to assess the future supply of workers.

Recruitment and Retention

Qualitative findings from the *EMS Workforce Assessment* stressed the importance of recruitment and retention to meeting the demand for EMS services. Concern about recruitment and retention issues was widespread; however, specific problems reported varied by geography. There was also substantial interest among key stakeholders about how to increase EMS workforce diversity. Other key qualitative findings included concern about low wages and lack of employee benefits, career ladders, and other means of promoting employee growth, advancement, and satisfaction. Little awareness of effective models for recruitment and retention were found.

Quantitative data from the Longitudinal Emergency Medical Technician Attributes and Demographics Study (LEADS) survey regarding workforce satisfaction and retention present a picture of a workforce that is fairly satisfied.[5] However, we know little about workers who leave a job to seek a position in another EMS agency or those who permanently leave the EMS workforce. The factors that impede or enhance career growth and worker development in the field need to be identified and shared. Without accurate information efforts to improve working conditions, recruit and retain more workers, and create more satisfying career models are likely to remain ineffective.

Management

The *EMS Workforce Assessment* revealed an industry-wide concern about the relationship between EMS managers and employees. Yet there is little to no evidence of training and education courses geared toward teaching EMS managers the fundamentals of leadership and organizational management. Results from the LEADS survey suggest that paramedics are less satisfied with their supervisors than EMTs.[5] The larger investment in time and education required for paramedics may cause them to form higher expectations of management. The management structure in EMS systems and the competency of EMS managers are important components of any long-term strategy to enhance worker retention.

Rural and Volunteer EMS Workforce

It is especially difficult to assess the issue of adequate distribution of EMS workers and other resources across geographic areas. The *EMS Workforce Assessment* found that in rural areas, issues of critical concern were: (1) the recruitment of an adequate number of workers; (2) the ability to offer compensation and incentives that will increase retention of workers, and (3) the overall rural EMS financing system. The sustainability of the rural EMS workforce must be addressed during implementation of the *EMS Workforce Agenda*.[4, 6]

The *EMS Workforce Assessment* also focused on the critical contribution of the volunteer EMS workforce in meeting demand for EMS services. Little is known about the size, distribution, composition, and demographics of the volunteer EMS workforce; or about factors related to satisfaction and retention among volunteers.[4, 7] Yet, there was general agreement that volunteers are, and will continue to be, an essential component of the EMS workforce, particularly in rural areas.

Health and Safety

Health and safety were major concerns identified in the *EMS Workforce Assessment*.[4] Many key informants expressed concern over what they perceived as a lack of emphasis in the field on following safety and injury prevention protocols. Some informants spoke of a need to develop a "culture of safety" in EMS, while others pointed to a strong concern over inadequate health insurance for workers in this high-risk field. In addition, there has been considerable attention from EMS researchers to the high rates of worker injury and the lack of systematic collection of worker illness and injury data.[8, 9, 10]

Compensation: Pay and Benefits

Pay and benefits were among the factors most frequently cited as having an impact on recruitment and retention. Most informants indicated that pay in the field is generally too low given the level and types of EMS worker responsibilities. Municipal and fire-based EMS services often have higher pay than hospital-based and private EMS services. Many informants believe that benefits, such as health insurance and retirement plans, are inadequate.

Salary data from the Bureau of Labor Statistics (BLS) support the perception that EMS workers receive relatively low compensation for their work. Comparisons of the median combined wages of EMTs/paramedics[1] to the wages of other public safety workers in 2005 showed that the median hourly wage was $12.54 for EMTs/paramedics, compared to $26.82 for firefighters and $22.25 for police/patrol officers.[4]

Analysis of LEADS data showed that 24.5% of EMTs lacked insurance coverage, compared to 9.6% of paramedics. Overall, 17.5% of EMS workers are without health insurance coverage.[4]

Professional Identity and Status

Most key informants interviewed for the *EMS Workforce Assessment* perceived the public as having favorable perceptions of EMS agencies and workers. However, there was a general perception that EMS has a low public profile compared to the fire service and that a portion of the public seem unaware that EMTs and paramedics have skills that are vitally important in emergency situations. Most informants thought the general visibility of EMS and the public's perception of the field influences the recruitment and retention potential of EMTs and paramedics.

---

[1] Recall that the BLS-OES data do not distinguish EMTs from paramedics.

COMPONENTS OF THE EMS WORKFORCE AGENDA

Development of the *EMS Workforce Agenda* included using the findings of the *EMS Workforce Assessment*, steering committee guidance, and input from a group of national stakeholders composed of EMS industry leaders; experts from professional organizations; educational and credentialing organizations; public and private providers; state and federal EMS agencies; and other stakeholder groups (see Appendix A). All levels of the national EMS community will continue to be involved throughout the implementation of the *EMS Workforce Agenda*.

The remainder of this document further defines and discusses the four essential components of the *EMS Workforce Agenda*. It examines the current status of each component ("where we are") and goals for each component ("where we want to be in the year 2020"). Each section includes proposed steps toward the achievement of the goals ("how to get there").

Health, Safety, and Wellness

The health, safety, and overall wellness of workers are essential for ensuring a capable and robust workforce. Given the nature of EMS work, EMTs and paramedics are vulnerable to serious, potentially fatal risks including, but not limited to, vehicle crashes, musculoskeletal injuries, infectious diseases, and assaults. Understanding the impact of these and other health risks on the ability of EMS systems to deliver high-quality prehospital health care is essential to EMS workforce planning. Furthermore, many EMS leaders would prefer to see more emphasis on the overall wellness of EMS workers. They would prefer workplace policies that foster a culture that supports the physical and mental health of EMS workers, and that encourages self-responsibility through on- and off-the-job behaviors which decrease the overall risk of illness and injury.

Where We Are

The *EMS Workforce Assessment* found that the health, safety, and wellness of EMS workers are of great concern. Key informant interviews revealed that many leaders believe that EMS workers, including managers, place inadequate emphasis on following on-the-job safety protocols. To a certain extent, this was attributed to overworked staff and overburdened agencies and systems. Several specific concerns cited include:

- Lack of evidence-based workplace safety precautions and procedures
- Inconsistent reporting of accidents, injuries, and "near-misses"
- Inconsistent emergency vehicle operations standards
- Lack of training in safe emergency vehicle operations
- Infrequent use of vehicle Event Data Recorders (e.g., black boxes), despite their high potential for revealing important information about the causes of ambulance crashes

National EMS and fire associations, as well as researchers, have brought more attention to EMS health and safety issues, such as scene safety, ambulance vehicle safety, seat belt use, infectious disease, hazardous material exposures, and physical fitness. However, evaluation of existing interventions and development of new interventions have lacked focused national attention. To date, there is no national level illness and injury surveillance program for EMS workers and there has been no comprehensive national assessment of EMS workforce health and safety. Experts interviewed for the *EMS Workforce Assessment* frequently cited illness and injury among EMS workers as a major workforce concern.[4]

A recent NHTSA sponsored project and report titled *Feasibility for an EMS Workforce Safety and Health Surveillance System* (2007)[3] provided substantial justification for developing a surveillance program for EMS illness and injury. Literature reviews conducted for the project found that the injury rate in EMS is high compared to other industries.[8] One study states that the occupational fatality rate for EMS workers was more than twice the national average.[9]

The feasibility report included several notable conclusions. Factors such as the unknown size of the EMS workforce and the variety of EMS organizational structures pose difficulties for comprehensive EMS health and injury surveillance. Various data systems were identified in the report, including the Census of Fatal Occupational Injuries,[21] the Fatal Analysis Reporting System,[22] and the National Electronic Injury Surveillance System.[23] The authors concluded that although these systems contribute to our understanding of EMS workforce illness and injury and could potentially contribute more, none of these individual systems can serve as a comprehensive source of surveillance data that is representative of the entire EMS workforce illness and injury profile. The report recommended that a comprehensive surveillance program should rely upon integrated data systems through which data could be shared and aggregated. EMS stakeholders were encouraged to work together with data managers to encourage analysis and dissemination of information on EMS workforce illnesses and injuries. Finally, the report recommended that a National EMS Workforce Injury and Illness Surveillance and Program (EMS-WIISP) be established with the ultimate goal of improving the health and safety of EMS workers.[3]

Where We Want To Be In 2020

In 2020, the health and safety of the EMS workforce will be an industry-wide priority. Injuries and illnesses affecting the workforce will be identified and understood such as causes, consequences and costs, and will be tracked through a national EMS workforce injury and illness surveillance program. The impact of illness and injury on the EMS workforce will be understood, including the health outcomes of workers, recruitment, retention, job performance, worker satisfaction, and EMS system costs. New threats to workforce health and safety, including those resulting from large-scale incidents, will be proactively identified and mitigated.

Effective intervention programs, guided by ongoing research and outcome evaluation will be developed and shared with the EMS community. Injury and illness prevention practices, including evidence-based, proactive risk-based strategies, will be fundamental to EMS systems at local, regional, state, and national levels. A culture of safety and wellness will exist within the workforce, where safe work practices will be continuously taught, performed, supported and evaluated by all members of the workforce, including management. The EMS community at large will place a high value on workforce wellness.

Local EMS systems and agencies will promote, by every means necessary, a culture of safety in EMS, including the development and use of best practices for worker health and safety. They will ensure that their workers are provided the necessary material resources and other support for following best practices in health and safety. Local EMS systems and agencies will report all worker illnesses and injuries consistent with nationally standardized methods and definitions.

State EMS agencies will continue their EMS workforce regulatory role and will also act as conduits for sharing information and resources with local EMS systems and agencies, including:

- Best practices for illness and injury prevention
- Best practices for worker wellness
- Material resources for illness and injury prevention and wellness programs
- Technical support for collection and management of illness and injury data

State EMS agencies will facilitate the collection and reporting of data on incidents of EMS personnel work-related illnesses and injuries.

An EMS-Workforce Injury and Illness Surveillance Program (EMS-WIISP) will exist at the national level and will coordinate the collection and the reporting of illness and injury data. The program will have sufficient resources for developing the data collection infrastructure and providing technical assistance to states.

How to Get There

Making EMS worker health, safety, and wellness a priority at all levels will require a better understanding of EMS worker illness and injury and appropriate intervention and prevention strategies. The first step is to create an integrated program for EMS occupational health and safety surveillance. Epidemiologists will use the data to evaluate and compare exposures and risk of illnesses, injuries, and fatalities to that of healthy and uninjured EMS workers. The EMS-WIISP will integrate data from existing surveillance systems to guide development of effective strategies to reduce the risk of illness and injury for the EMS workforce. Local, state, and national strategies will be developed for surveillance, intervention, evaluation, and prevention efforts.

The EMS-WIISP will be guided by the findings and goals of the *National Occupational Research Agenda: National Public Safety Sub-Sector Agenda for Occupational Safety and Health Research and Practice in the U.S.*[24] Continual surveillance of EMS workforce health and safety is necessary to guide and direct intervention strategies. This will assist with the prioritization of prevention efforts (at the local, state, and national levels) and enable the mitigation of potential new risks to workforce health and safety. Regular literature reviews of relevant topics and feedback from individual workers, managers, and experts should be conducted to ensure a complete assessment of the workforce health status. The EMS-WIISP will contribute to ensuring a healthy and safe EMS workforce for the future.

An effective program of illness and injury surveillance, including research, should be the basis for an EMS workforce illness and injury profile, and should include data such as:

- Types and prevalence of illness and injury
- Incidence of disability and mortality
- Etiology of illness and injury
- Workforce demographics
- "Near-miss" incidents

- Vehicle crash-related morbidity and mortality

Evidence-based prevention controls and strategies should be implemented. Fundamental research questions that should be routinely addressed include, for instance:

- Risk of experiencing illness and injury
- Impact of illness and injury upon the workforce and the overall EMS industry, including:
  - Recruitment
  - Retention and turnover
  - Economic cost to industry

In addition to funding and research a culture of EMS workplace safety and wellness should be cultivated. For example, the policies, procedures, training, and programs in industries with similar dynamic risk profiles, such as trucking, shipping, mining and agriculture may be shared and evaluated with EMS to establish clear workforce safety practices and procedures. Successful wellness programs should be identified and tailored to the EMS community. Regular forums for sharing best practices with provider groups should be established. Awareness of the culture of safety should be extended into educational programs so that new workers would enter the field with a broader appreciation for their own safety and well-being and that of their peers.

Additionally, the EMS industry should commit to implementing the strategic goals set forth from the report of the National Public Safety Sub-Sector Agenda for Occupational Safety and Health Research and Practice in the U.S.[24] This sub-sector group of the National Occupational Research Agenda (NORA) identified five strategic goals for Emergency Medical Services:

- "Reduce traumatic injury and fatalities among EMS personnel associated with vehicle crashes…"
- "Reduce traumatic injuries among EMS personnel that occur during movement of patients and equipment…"
- "Reduce hazardous exposures to EMS personnel through effective design and use of PPE, and proper work practices…"
- "Identify and implement effective policies among EMS agencies regarding work organization factors to reduce related illnesses and injuries…"

- "Create an integrated occupational health and safety surveillance data system for Emergency Medical Service (EMS) personnel and evaluate risks for their exposures, illnesses, injuries, and fatalities…"

The NORA document also includes several intermediate goals, such as improving EMS vehicle design and developing guidelines for EMS worksite medical surveillance and wellness programs.

Education and Certification

EMS is dependent upon its education programs to produce graduates with the educational foundation to become highly competent workers. Changes in the EMS education system may impact the availability of workers. In June 2000, NHTSA initiated a major effort to restructure EMS education with the release of the *EMS Education Agenda for the Future: A Systems Approach*.[2] The *EMS Education Agenda* is discussed in more detail below.

Where We Are

The state of EMS education in the United States is difficult to assess because of inadequate data and variability across states. NHTSA's National Standard Curricula have provided a common framework for EMS education; however, consistency across states has not yet been achieved. The majority of states require National Registry of Emergency Medical Technicians (NREMT) initial certification at both the EMT and paramedic levels. Several other states require certification at one level or the other, while five do not require NREMT certification at all.[4] There is also considerable interstate variability in state policies regarding recertification, continuing education and continued competency. The lack of interstate consistency is reflected in the differing scopes of practice and job titles or licensure categories.

The quality of EMS education varies considerably from program to program and state to state.[12] Variations in EMS education, certification and licensing make it difficult for EMTs and paramedics to move easily across state lines. The absence of seamless reciprocity could make an EMS career less attractive to potential recruits and may impact the ability of EMS workers to respond to a large-scale disaster across state lines.

The major objective of the *EMS Education Agenda* is to establish a national system of EMS education similar to that which exists for most other allied health professions. The *EMS Education Agenda* includes five components. Three of these components have been completed: the *National EMS Core Content*[13] describes the entire domain of out-of-hospital care; the *National EMS Scope of Practice Model*[14] defines the levels and entry-level competencies of prehospital EMS providers, and the *National EMS Education Standards*[15]. The two other components, still not fully implemented throughout the nation, are National EMS Education Program Accreditation and National EMS Certification.

Although the *EMS Education Agenda* addresses obstacles to becoming employed across state lines, it does not address the obstacles to responding to large-scale, out of jurisdiction emergencies. In 2004, the Department of Homeland Security (DHS) released its plan for a National Incident Management System (NIMS).[16] NIMS is a comprehensive approach to emergency incident management that requires all public and private sector personnel "with a direct role in emergency management and response"[17] to become certified through the National Emergency Responder Credentialing System, "NIMS credentialing," which is currently under development. NIMS credentialing will entail meeting minimum standards for education, training, competencies, and other qualifications of various emergency response professions, and it will allow for quick verification of the credentials of emergency response personnel in the event of a cross-jurisdictional incident.[18]

Where We Want To Be In 2020

In 2020, the EMS education system will be nationally integrated. EMS workers will have the ability to move across state lines and obtain EMS employment with minimal disruption due to successful implementation of the *EMS Education Agenda.* There will be a nationally uniform process for assuring ongoing EMS professional competency. Personnel will be educated to provide culturally competent care including care for diverse groups such as children, the elderly, the disabled (who have special medical needs and may also require specialized medical equipment), and patients with limited English proficiency. There will be a system that permits nationally certified, state licensed EMS workers to respond across jurisdictional lines in the event of large-scale emergencies. Pertinent data on all EMS education programs and graduates will be tracked at the state and national levels, allowing for estimates of the future workforce supply. EMS educators will be certified to ensure their graduates will possess the knowledge, competencies, and skills to provide high quality EMS care.

How to Get There

The Institute of Medicine's Committee on the Future of Emergency Care in the United States Health System stated its support for the goals of the *EMS Education Agenda* in a 2006 report.[12] Nationwide implementation of the *EMS Education Agenda*[2] is of critical importance, requiring support from a broad range of EMS stakeholder agencies and organizations and should include:

- A national accreditation requirement for all paramedic programs that will be recognized and required by all states
- A phase-in plan for national accreditations of all EMS programs
- The reporting of enrollment and graduation data from all EMS education programs to the National Center for Education Statistics (NCES) or other national data repository
- Verification of the knowledge, skills, abilities and competencies of all EMS providers, through national certification, that is the basis for licensure in all states
- Common scopes of practice, titling, and licensure categories for EMS workers across states
- Grants and technical assistance to assist states and education programs implement the *EMS Education Agenda*
- Re-certification that is national, and with common requirements across states that will serve as the basis for achieving reciprocity
- An EMS education infrastructure that is supported at the state and federal levels

In conjunction with the *EMS Education Agenda*, the NIMS National Emergency Responder Credentialing System is needed. A NIMS credential, based upon state EMS licensure and the national EMS certification, will better enable EMS workers to respond to cross-jurisdictional emergencies. Preparedness education should be integrated into the National EMS Education Standards. Funding support of accredited EMS education programs will better enable preparedness education of EMS workers.

EMS education programs should be nationally accredited, State licensure laws/regulations should be consistent with the National EMS Scope of Practice Model, and states should use National EMS Certification as a basis for EMS state licensure. Education programs should report data to the National Center for Education Statistics (NCES) or other comparable national body.

There should be nationwide implementation of NIMS credentialing[19] that is linked to implementation of the *EMS Education Agenda*. The development of the EMS educational infrastructure must be supported at the federal level. Educator credentialing and maintenance of national EMS certification are essential elements in enhancing the professionalism of EMS workers.

Data and Research

Because they provide the foundation for evidence-based workforce planning, workforce data and research are essential to ensuring a capable and robust EMS workforce for the future. Currently EMS workforce data exists in a variety of forms including research or technical organizations that warehouse data; academic databases of independently collected data, and administrative databases, such as licensing boards and private organizations (e.g. certification boards). Workforce research often includes scientifically designed studies as well as less rigorous market surveys. Just as clinical research is necessary to guide patient care protocols and clinical decision making, workforce research is necessary to guide planning for workforce development.

Where We Are

The *National EMS Research Agenda* (*EMS Research Agenda*) identifies "two primary barriers that have inhibited the development of a strong research program in EMS: a paucity of well trained researchers with an interest in EMS research and a lack of reliable funding sources to support research."[11] According to the *EMS Workforce Assessment*[4] "there is a paucity of EMS workforce data and research." Until we have more fundamental knowledge about the EMS workforce, most of the other components of this workforce agenda will be difficult to address.

The *EMS Workforce Assessment*[4] found that much of the data necessary for evaluating the adequacy of EMS workforce supply flawed or unavailable. The size of the existing workforce is unknown due primarily to a lack of information about volunteer EMS workers and cross-trained firefighter-EMTs. Similarly, it is not known how many students are in the educational pipeline to become EMS workers because there is not a central information source on education providers.

The gaps and inadequacies in knowledge about the EMS workforce are striking in comparison to what is known about other public safety and health care professions. These shortcomings can have major consequences for the EMS workforce. Current national estimates may undercount the workforce and therefore may not accurately predict future demand for EMS workers.

The National Emergency Medical Services Information System (NEMSIS)[2] is a major effort to establish a nationwide network for the collection of EMS patient and system data. It has established two datasets – the Demographics Dataset and the EMS Dataset. The first contains demographic variables for EMS agencies, while the EMS Dataset includes information that describes a complete EMS prehospital patient care incident.

Prior to the implementation of NEMSIS, national data on EMS incidents were scarce thus imposing a general limitation on EMS research. Although NEMSIS was not specifically developed with the objective of increasing and improving EMS workforce research, the data collected could greatly enhance the ability to assess the impact of workforce factors such as ambulance staffing configuration on patient outcomes.

Where We Want To Be In 2020

In 2020, basic EMS workforce data, including workforce size and compensation information, will be known and accessible. In addition to data on these broad characteristics, there will be a source for comprehensive, current, and accurate data on the EMS workforce and its characteristics at the local, state, and national levels. These data will be updated regularly and will include, as a minimum, the following:

- Workforce size and demographics
- Workforce composition
    - Practice levels
    - Volunteer and paid workforce
- Pipeline/educational program enrollees and graduates
- Certification and licensure status
- Worker health and safety
- Retention and turnover rates
- Compensation

In 2020, there will be a cadre of well trained researchers – including some with backgrounds as EMS providers – who will specialize in EMS workforce studies. To support and maintain this development, formal mentorship programs in EMS workforce research will be created. These programs will include research fellowships at academic, research, and professional organizations. In addition, federal support will be increased and relevant agencies will be actively engaged in addressing workforce issues.

---

[2] Sponsoring organizations are NHTSA, CDC, HRSA, University of Utah, UNC Chapel Hill.

There will be widespread dissemination of the *EMS Research Agenda* and resources will be made available to researchers, including a regularly updated list of potential grant and funding sources for EMS workforce research, a list of top research priorities and an annual index of EMS workforce research publications.

Local EMS agencies will incorporate workforce data into their information systems and also routinely provide workforce data to their state EMS offices. Local EMS educational programs will regularly provide educational data to their state EMS offices. Local EMS leaders will use research to guide policy and workforce planning.

State EMS offices will have systems to collect data from local agencies and educational institutions and to report a subset of that data at the national level. Examples include demographic characteristics, educational background, system configuration, recruitment, retention, turnover, and injury and illness statistics. State EMS officials will have a clear understanding of the importance of workforce research in guiding local, state, and national EMS workforce assessments. States will provide tools and resources, based on national templates for best practices, to guide local agencies in the use of data, research, and workforce planning.

There will be a comprehensive national EMS workforce dataset. To ensure that the data are compatible with other national EMS data sources, uniform inclusion criteria and definitions will be developed. Data templates will be made available to states as teaching tools for data collection and management, and workforce research and planning.

Data from the Bureau of Labor Statistics (BLS) will more accurately represent the composition of the EMS workforce including the volunteer workforce. A reliable stream of funding for EMS workforce research will be available from government agencies, foundations, non-profit organizations, professional associations, and private sources. There will be qualified researchers prepared to ask and address important research questions, and they will be able to draw on national workforce datasets to frame and answer these research questions. EMS workforce research will be disseminated throughout national, state, and local EMS organizations.

How to Get There

The EMS community must continue to coordinate with the Bureau of Labor Statistics (BLS), the National Center for Education Statistics (NCES), and other agencies to improve national data collection, estimates of EMS workforce size, and projections of future workforce supply and demand. For example, improvements to current BLS data should distinguish EMTs from paramedics and identify EMS workers who are cross-trained and working in fire-based or other systems.

Improving the quality and scope of EMS workforce data will take a national effort. Stakeholders must increase their awareness of the need for quality EMS workforce data and participate in the development of a data collection network. To improve knowledge about the size, composition, and location of the EMS workforce, it is critical to develop and implement a universally shared set of EMS workforce data terms and definitions that, at a minimum, adequately account for: (1) volunteerism in EMS; (2) EMS workers trained as firefighters, and (3) EMS workers in the allied health fields.

The quality and scope of EMS education program data needs improvement. EMS education programs should be nationally accredited and regularly provide data to national agencies such as the National Center for Education Statistics (NCES). A national effort will be needed to lead the development of common data definitions for educational programs and graduates. Data definitions should address public, proprietary, and agency-based education programs, as well as both EMT and paramedic programs. Educational issues are discussed more extensively in the education section of this document.

To promote the value of EMS workforce research for effective workforce planning to local, state, and national EMS organizations, the following steps must be taken:

- Develop a cadre of researchers with excellent research skills and an appropriate background in EMS to conduct ongoing EMS workforce research
- Develop reliable funding sources for EMS workforce research through advocacy with government agencies, foundations, non-profit organizations, professional associations, and private sources[11, 3]
- Create a searchable index of EMS workforce research that will be available to researchers and local, state, and federal stakeholders.

---

[3] The National EMS Research Agenda proposes the following: "Additional annual funding in an amount equal to 1% of the annual expenditure on EMS systems should be allocated for research into the effectiveness of those systems. This would mean approximately $50 million would be available for research each year."

Workforce Planning and Development

Workforce planning is the process of turning what is known about a workforce into plans, activities, and tools that help ensure enough workers are available to meet the demand of each practice level. At its core, workforce planning is a methodical process of measuring the difference in magnitude between the current workforce and the predicted future demand for workers. Based on the size of this difference, steps should be taken by local agencies, systems, and states to meet the future demand for workers. Workforce planning can also account for other important factors such as the types of skills that will be required to meet a population's EMS needs and how emerging technologies will impact changes in the roles and demands of EMS workers.

Where We Are

Key informant interviews demonstrate that leaders in the field are worried about the continuing viability of the EMS workforce. Workforce shortages are the most consistently identified workforce concern of EMS employers. There is also concern with issues such as recruitment, retention, diversity and having enough workers to fulfill the mission of providing quality emergency care. Many employers express frustration over an inability to compensate their workers appropriately due to systemic barriers in EMS system funding and reimbursement. Despite these concerns, local agencies/systems and state EMS agencies receive little guidance on workforce planning.

The *EMS Workforce Assessment* suggests that there has been more success with recruitment than retention, as little is known about why workers leave the EMS field. In general, a "big picture" concept of workforce planning, based on an understanding of workforce supply and demand is largely absent from the EMS field. Workforce planning is not a common subject of EMS literature and the *EMS Workforce Assessment* revealed no systematic workforce planning approach in the EMS industry. Local agencies and systems, and some states, have attempted to address their workforce needs with little guidance on workforce planning, but express frustration due to the lack of workforce planning models or best practices. In particular, little information exists on strategies for the recruitment and retention of volunteers. Key informants expressed a desire to know more about what motivates people to volunteer as EMTs and what factors make recruitment and retention more likely. As an example, some volunteers are compensated through receipt of benefits or stipends, but it is not known how many volunteers are compensated or if compensation has a relationship with recruitment and retention.

Workforce planning has been used for decades within industry and business, and more recently has been widely used in government. The National Academy of Public Administration (NAPA), an organization chartered by Congress to improve government at all levels, outlined the importance of government workforce planning in a May 2000 white paper - *Building Successful Organizations: A Guide to Strategic Workforce Planning*[20]. Many public and private organizations have developed their own workforce planning models. Aside from variations in terminology, the processes are similar. Most workforce planning models include factors such as:

- Current data on workforce supply (number of workers; number of students in pipeline) and demand (vacancy and turnover rates)
- Worker compensation, including pay, benefits, and other incentives
- "Environmental" factors, including:
    - Geographic factors and population demographics that impact need for EMS services;
    - Regulations;
    - Numbers and types of other providers in the region.
- Economics and cost analysis, including budget considerations
- Evaluation of the workforce planning model to determine that organizational objectives are being met

Where We Want To Be In 2020

In 2020, EMS provider organizations will be aware of best practices for workforce planning and will have the tools necessary for implementation. Local EMS providers and systems will receive workforce planning tools from their state EMS offices and technical assistance on their use. EMS workforce research will have produced valid information on important issues such as:

- Recruitment
- Retention
- Initial and continuing education and training
- Workforce diversity
- Use of volunteer workers
- Compensation (including compensation of volunteers)
- Assessment of future supply and demand
- Assessment of changing roles
- Impact of changing technology
- Staffing configurations and patient outcomes
- Staffing configurations and job satisfaction

Local EMS systems and agencies will be familiar with concepts of workforce planning and EMS managers will have access to workforce planning guides, tools, and expertise through their state EMS offices and a national EMS workforce technical assistance center. EMS managers will be able to recognize and meet the EMS needs of special populations, such as children, the elderly, the disabled, and patients with limited English proficiency. They will also be able to analyze local EMS workforce supply and demand and identify gaps between the present supply and demand and estimated future needs. Local EMS systems and agencies will be able to prepare plans to eliminate gaps and build the needed future workforce. They will be aware of potential workforce problems before patient care is negatively impacted. Local EMS systems and agencies will have access to information on best practices in recruitment, retention, and planning. With ready access to state and national EMS workforce data they will be able to monitor trends and compare their local issues with state and national workforce issues.

Workforce planning will be understood and promoted by state EMS offices. State EMS officials will use the broad principles of workforce planning to guide planning in their states. In cooperation with national workforce resources, states will disseminate educational programs, materials, guides, tools, and resources among EMS agencies to assist with local workforce planning.

There will be a broad understanding of EMS workforce planning and the dynamics and application of the following workforce issues:

- Supply, demand, and resource needs
- Pipeline assessment
- Workforce turnover, recruitment, and retention
- Effective models for projecting workforce need

Government and private EMS organizations will support workforce planning by assisting in the education of states and local agencies in workforce planning and supporting national workforce data collection and research.

How to Get There

At a national level systematic workforce planning should be demonstrated as a vital practice for ensuring a robust and capable EMS workforce and for promoting the value of the EMS profession. State EMS offices should engage in the following activities:

- Fund workforce planning resources including the provision of workforce planning education to local systems and agencies
- Assist in the identification of workforce planning best practices
- Support workforce planning by helping local agencies obtain necessary data and statistics
- Use statewide data to project trends and potential future demands

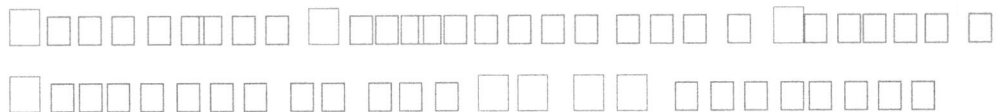

The National EMS Workforce Technical Assistance Center (TAC) will facilitate the systematic collection of national EMS workforce data. It will provide guidance in the development of the four essential components of the *EMS Workforce Agenda*, especially as they relate to the collection, management, and use of EMS workforce data. The TAC will facilitate research regarding EMS workforce issues by facilitating researcher access to common sources of EMS data. It will also facilitate communication among various stakeholders in the collection and use of EMS workforce data. Stakeholders include:

- EMS workers
- EMS employers
- State EMS offices
- Local and tribal EMS systems and provider agencies
- Certification and accreditation organizations

- Education programs and institutions
- National, state, and local EMS organizations
- Federal EMS agencies
- Public health agencies
- Private EMS providers
- Rural health agencies

The TAC will increase awareness of the need for current and accurate data and will provide technical assistance to improve EMS workforce data quality. The TAC will participate in efforts to improve national EMS workforce injury and illness surveillance. Finally, the TAC will function as a clearinghouse of information on EMS workforce research, including information on upcoming and new research projects, as well as providing access to the findings from completed studies

Figure 1 of this document describes the four essential components of the *EMS Workforce Agenda* presented in relation to each other and to the proposed National EMS Workforce Technical Assistance Center (TAC). The four components of the *EMS Workforce Agenda* are:

- Worker health, safety, and wellness
- Education and certification
- Data and research
- Workforce planning and development

These four components form a mutually reinforcing system. Workforce data and research are of particular importance for facilitating the implementation of each component. Comprehensive, current, and accurate workforce data provide the foundation for empirical research on all aspects of the workforce. The coordinated efforts from all EMS stakeholders are integral toward advancing the vision of the *EMS Workforce Agenda*.

The *EMS Workforce Agenda* is an ambitious undertaking involving complex components and numerous groups of stakeholders. It sets forth a vision for a well educated, adequately prepared, and appropriately credentialed EMS workforce that is valued, well compensated, healthy and safe.

The struggle to maintain a workforce of adequate size, with the exemplary skills needed to meet higher demand for services, has led EMS agencies to seek new approaches for recruiting, training, and retaining their workers. The EMS community has recognized the importance of taking a proactive and evidence-based approach to planning for a capable and robust EMS workforce and has called for a renewed emphasis on workforce health and safety. The *EMS Workforce Assessment* was the first major step towards realizing this goal. The *EMS Workforce Agenda* is the second major step in this process.

EMS stakeholders throughout the nation assisted with the development of this Agenda's vision and strategy. The *EMS Workforce Agenda* will assist EMS leaders in making informed decisions as they advance the future of the EMS profession.

Attendees at EMS Workforce Stakeholders Meeting

🗆 🖿🖿🖿🖿🖿🖿🖿🖿🖿🖿	🗆🗆🗆 🗆
American Academy of Pediatrics (AAP)	Bruce Klein
American Ambulance Association (AAA)	Jim Buell
American College of Emergency Physicians (ACEP)	David Schoenwetter
American College of Surgeons (ACS)	Michael Rotondo
Association of Air Medical Services (AAMS)	Gloria Dow
Emergency Nurses Association (ENA)	Melanie Standon
International Association of Fire Chiefs (IAFC)	John S. Butler
International Association of Fire Fighters (IAFF)	Jonathan Moore
National Association of EMS Educators (NAEMSE)	Angel Burba
National Association of EMS Physicians (NAEMSP)	John McManus
National Association of Emergency Medical Technicians (NAEMT)	Jerry Johnston
National Association of State EMS Officials	Robert Bass
National EMS Management Association (NEMSMA)	Chris Colangelo
National Registry of EMTs (NREMT)	Bill Brown
National Rural Health Association (NRHA)	Chris Tilden
National Volunteer Fire Council (NVFC)	Ken Knipper
Rural EMS and Trauma Technical Assistance Center (REMSTTAC)	Joseph Hansen

□□□□□□□ □□□□□□	□□□ □
CDC/NCIPC/Division of Injury Response (DIR)	Vik Kapil
DHS/Office of the Chief Medical Officer (CMO)	Jeffrey Runge & Joseph F. Martin, III
HRSA/EMS for Children National Resource Center	Jim Morehead
HRSA/Office of Rural Health Policy (ORHP)	Eileen Holloran
Indian Health Service EMS Program	Betty Hastings
DOT/NHTSA/Office of EMS	Drew Dawson
DOT/NHTSA/Office of EMS	Gamunu Wijetunge

Steering Committee

John Becknell
Roger Levine
Gregg Margolis
Richard Patrick
Ed Wetzel

University of California, San Francisco

Susan Chapman
Vanessa Lindler
Jennifer Kaiser

Facilitator
Robert Kingon

Additional Guests
National Registry of EMTs – Jimm Murray

NEMSIS Technical Assistance Center - David Owens

Virginia Department of Health: Office of EMS - Scott Winston

☐☐F☐☐☐☐C☐S

[1] National Highway Traffic Safety Administration. (1996). *Emergency Medical Services Agenda for the Future* (No. DOT HS 808 441). Washington, DC: U.S. Department of Transportation.

[2] National Highway Traffic Safety Administration. (2000). *EMS Education Agenda for the Future: A Systems Approach* (No. DOT HS 809 042). Washington, DC: U.S. Department of Transportation.

[3] Becker, L. R., & Spicer, R. (2007). *Feasibility for an EMS Workforce Safety and Health Surveillance System* (No. Contract DTNH22-05-D-25043). Washington, DC: National Highway Traffic Safety Administration.

[4] National Highway Traffic Safety Administration. (2008). *EMS Workforce for the 21st Century: A National Assessment* (No. DOT HS 810 943). Washington, DC: U.S. Department of Transportation.

[5] Brown, W. E., Jr., Dawson, D., & Levine, R. (2003). Compensation, benefits, and satisfaction: the Longitudinal Emergency Medical Technician Demographic Study (LEADS) Project. *Prehosp Emerg Care, 7*(3), 357-362.

[6] Office of Rural Health Policy. (2006). *Emergency Medical Services in Frontier Areas: Volunteer Community Organizations* (No. Contract Number HHSH250200436014C). Rockville, MD: Health Resources and Services Administration.

[7] Office of Rural Health Policy. (2000). *Challenges of Rural Emergency Medical Services - An Opinion Survey of State EMS Directors*. Rockville, MD: Health Resources and Services Administration.

[8] Maguire, B. J., Hunting, K. L., Guidotti, T. L., & Smith, G. S. (2005). Occupational injuries among emergency medical services personnel. *Prehosp Emerg Care, 9*(4), 405-411.

[9] Maguire, B. J., Hunting, K. L., Smith, G. S., & Levick, N. R. (2002). Occupational fatalities in emergency medical services: a hidden crisis. *Ann Emerg Med, 40*(6), 625-632.

[10] Bobick, T. G., Proudfoot, S. L., Romano, N. T., Moore, P. H., Current, R. S., & Green, J. D. (2003). Ambulance crash-related injuries among EMS workers, *National Occupational Injury Research Symposium*. Pittsburgh, PA.

[11] *National EMS Research Agenda*. (2001). from http://www.researchagenda.org/Documents/EMSResearchAgenda.pdf

[12] Committee on the Future of Emergency Care in the United States Health System. (2007). *Emergency Medical Services: At the Crossroads*. Washington, DC: The National Academies Press.

[13] National Highway Traffic Safety Administration. (2005). *National EMS Core Content*. Retrieved April 21, 2006, from http://www.nhtsa.dot.gov/people/injury/ems/EMSCoreContent/index.htm

[14] National Highway Traffic Safety Administration. (2006). *National EMS Scope of Practice Model* (No. DOT HS 810 657). Washington, DC: U.S. Department of Transportation.

[15] National Highway Traffic Safety Administration. (2008). *National EMS Education Standards*. Retrieved March, 2008, from http://www.nemses.org/draftstandards.html

[16] NIMSOnline.Com. (2004). *National Incident Management System (NIMS) FAQ*, from http://www.nimsonline.com/nims_faq.htm

[17] National Incident Management System Resource Center. (2008). *NIMS/NIC Training Frequently Asked Questions*. Retrieved April, 2008, from http://www.fema.gov/emergency/nims/faq/training.shtm

[18] National Incident Management System Resource Center. (2007). *Resource Management: Credentialing*. Retrieved April, 2008, from http://www.fema.gov/emergency/nims/rm/credentialing.shtm

[19] The NIMS Integration Center. (2005). *Credentialing FAQ's*, from http://www.nimsonline.com/docs/credent_faq.pdf

[20] Center for Human Resources Management. (2000). *Building Successful Organizations: A Guide to Strategic Workforce Planning*. Washington, DC: National Academy of Public Administration.

[21] Bureau of Labor Statistics. *Census of Fatal Occupational Injuries*. Retrieved April 29, 2008, from http://www.bls.gov/iif/oshcfoi1.htm

[22] National Highway Traffic Safety Administration. *Fatal Analysis Reporting System*. Retrieved April 29, 2008, from http://www-fars.nhtsa.dot.gov/Main/index.aspx

[23] U.S. Consumer Product Safety Commission. *National Electronic Injury Surveillance System*. Retrieved April 29, 2008, from http://www.cpsc.gov/cpscpub/pubs/3002.html

[24] National Institute for Occupational Safety and Health. (2008). *National Occupational Research Agenda: National Public Safety Sub-Sector Agenda for Occupational Safety and Health Research and Practice in the U.S.* (Draft Preliminary Public Comment Version). Washington, DC: Centers for Disease Control and Prevention.

www.ingramcontent.com/pod-product-compliance
Lightning Source LLC
Chambersburg PA
CBHW081156280526
45787CB00008B/3355